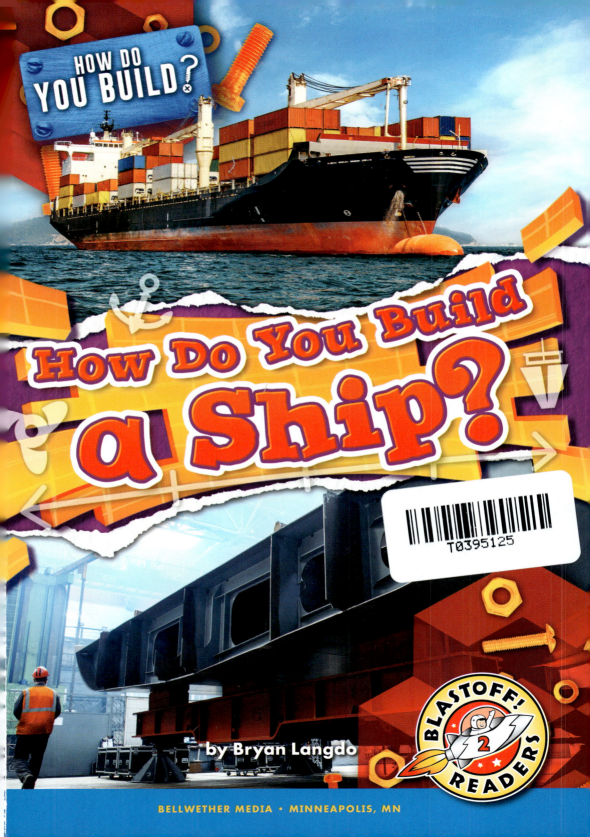

How Do You Build a Ship?

by Bryan Langdo

BLASTOFF! READERS

BELLWETHER MEDIA • MINNEAPOLIS, MN

Blastoff! Readers are carefully developed by literacy experts to build reading stamina and move students toward fluency by combining standards-based content with developmentally appropriate text.

LEVELS

Level 1 provides the most support through repetition of high-frequency words, light text, predictable sentence patterns, and strong visual support.

Level 2 offers early readers a bit more challenge through varied sentences, increased text load, and text-supportive special features.

Level 3 advances early-fluent readers toward fluency through increased text load, less reliance on photos, advancing concepts, longer sentences, and more complex special features.

★ **Blastoff! Universe**

Reading Level

Grade K

Grades 1–3

Grade 4

This edition first published in 2026 by Bellwether Media, Inc.

No part of this publication may be reproduced in whole or in part without written permission of the publisher. For information regarding permission, write to Bellwether Media, Inc., Attention: Permissions Department, 3500 American Blvd W, Suite 150, Bloomington, MN 55431.

Library of Congress Cataloging-in-Publication Data

LC record for How Do You Build a Ship? available at: https://lccn.loc.gov/2025010702

Text copyright © 2026 by Bellwether Media, Inc. BLASTOFF! READERS and associated logos are trademarks and/or registered trademarks of Bellwether Media, Inc. Bellwether Media is a division of FlutterBee Education Group.

Editor: Rachael Barnes   Book Designer: Josh Brink

Printed in the United States of America, North Mankato, MN.

Table of Contents

On the Ocean	4
Planning a Ship	6
At the Shipyard	8
Setting Out	20
Glossary	22
To Learn More	23
Index	24

On the Ocean

Happy people board a ship. Tugboats slowly pull it from the dock.

The ship sets out across the ocean!

tugboat

Planning a Ship

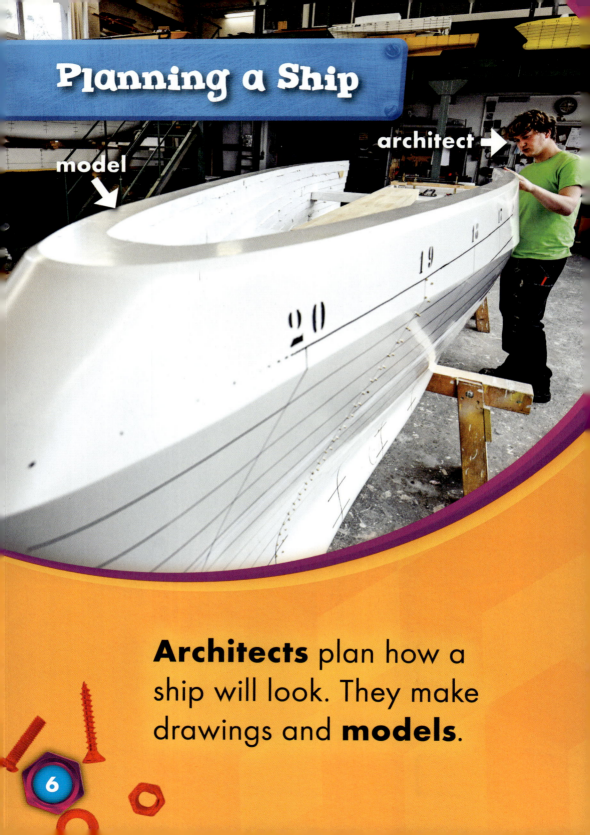

model

architect

Architects plan how a ship will look. They make drawings and **models**.

Engineers plan how the ship will run.

engineer

At the Shipyard

shipyard

welding

Ships are built in **shipyards**. Steel plates are cut and pressed into shapes.

Workers and robots **weld** the plates together. Cranes and trucks carry the pieces to a **dry dock**.

What Do You Need?

steel

blocks

cranes

The pieces sit on blocks.
They are welded together.
This makes the **hull**.

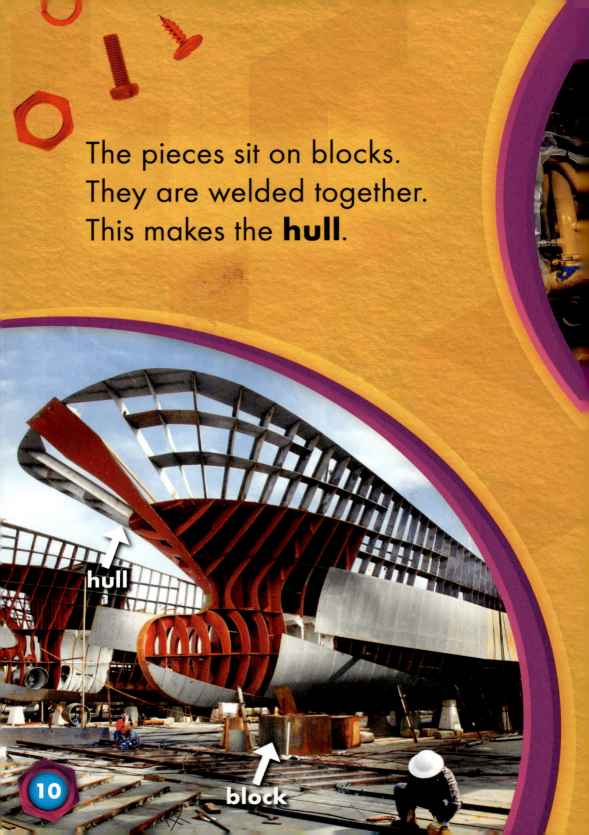

engine room

Workers make sure each piece is sealed. Next, engines and tanks go into the hull.

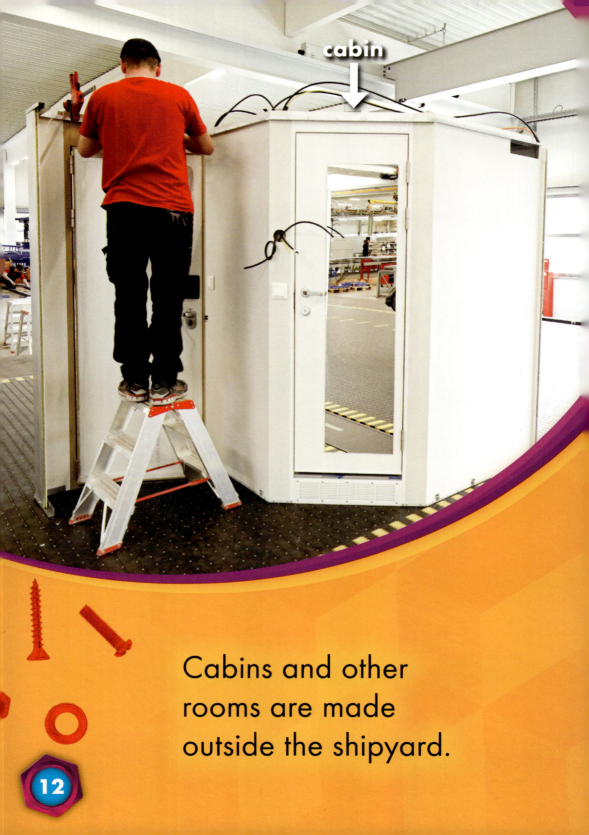

cabin

Cabins and other rooms are made outside the shipyard.

They are brought to the shipyard. Cranes move them into place.

Parts of a Ship

Workers build **decks**. They put in **propellers** and **anchors**.

The **bridge** is on the highest deck. Computers on the bridge help steer the ship.

propeller →

dry dock

ship lobby

This ship is ready for water. The dry dock is filled with water. The ship floats!

Workers finish the inside of the ship.

Icon of the Seas

Company	Royal Caribbean International
Year completed	2024
Length	1,196 feet (365 meters)
Weight	around 250,000 tons (226,796 metric tons)
Famous for	biggest cruise ship in the world

17

It is time for **sea trials**. These test the ship's safety and how it moves in water.

Step by Step

1. Workers plan the ship.

2. Workers and robots weld steel plates.

3. Workers add engines and tanks.

4. The ship gets decks and cabins.

5. Water fills the dry dock.

6. Sea trials test the ship.

Workers make any needed changes. Now the ship is ready to sail!

Setting Out

Some ships take people on vacation. Others carry goods across oceans.

Ships connect people around the world!

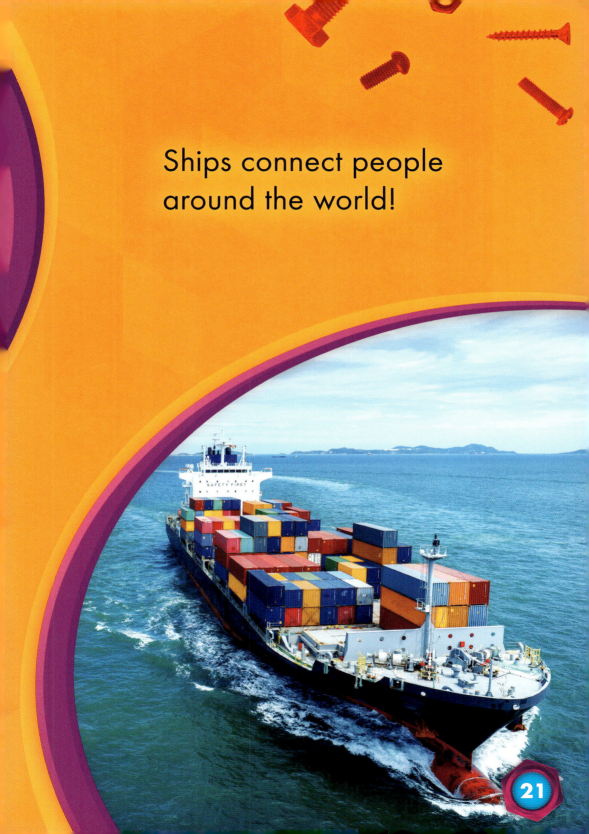

Glossary

anchors—devices that are attached to a ship and dropped into water to hold the ship in place

architects—people who design ships and other structures

bridge—a room from which a ship is directed

decks—flat parts on the tops of ships

dry dock—a special dock in a shipyard where water can be pumped in and out while a ship is being built or repaired

engineers—people who are trained to design and build machines, systems, or structures

hull—the main body of a ship

models—small versions of ships or other structures; models can be physical or digital.

propellers—parts with blades that are turned by an engine to make something move

sea trials—tests done on the ocean to make sure a ship is working properly and safely

shipyards—places where ships are built or repaired

weld—to join pieces together by melting metal

To Learn More

AT THE LIBRARY

Crestodina, Tom. *Working Boats: An Inside Look at Ten Amazing Watercraft.* Seattle, Wash.: Little Bigfoot, 2022.

Duling, Kaitlyn. *Cruise Ships.* Minneapolis, Minn.: Bellwether Media, 2026.

Schmitt, Kelly Rice. *I Ship: A Container Ship's Colossal Journey.* Minneapolis, Minn.: Millbrook Press, 2023.

ON THE WEB

FACTSURFER

Factsurfer.com gives you a safe, fun way to find more information.

1. Go to www.factsurfer.com.

2. Enter "ship" into the search box and click 🔍.

3. Select your book cover to see a list of related content.

Index

anchors, 14
architects, 6
blocks, 10
bridge, 14, 15
cabins, 12
computers, 14
cranes, 9, 13
decks, 14
dock, 4
drawings, 6
dry dock, 9, 16
engineers, 7
engines, 11
hull, 10, 11
Icon of the Seas, 17
models, 6
ocean, 4, 20
parts of a ship, 13
pieces, 9, 10, 11

propellers, 14
robots, 9
sea trials, 18
shipyards, 8, 12, 13
steel plates, 8, 9
step by step, 19
tanks, 11
trucks, 9
tugboats, 4
weld, 8, 9, 10
what do you need?, 9
workers, 9, 11, 14, 17, 19

The images in this book are reproduced through the courtesy of: Federico Rostagno, cover (top hero); Dmitry Markov152, cover (bottom hero); VIKTOR KHYMYCH, pp. 2-3; Ceri Breeze, p. 4; mariakray, pp. 4-5; Jens Kalaene/ AP Images, p. 6; Steve Welsh/ Getty Images, p. 7; Dwayne Senior/ Bloomberg/ Getty Images, pp. 8, 11; Bradley C. Bower/ Bloomberg / Getty Images, p. 8 (welding); Laurentiu Iordache, p. 9 (steel); Jose Gil, p. 9 (blocks); Kirill Neiezhmakov, p. 9 (cranes); Liu Zhenqing/ VCG/ Getty Images, p. 10; Bernd W'stneck/ picture-alliance/ dpa/ AP Images, p. 12; Kirk Fisher, p. 13 (cabin); Wirestock Creators, p. 13 (propeller); Alexey Seafarer, p. 13 (engine); NAN728, p. 13 (ship); Alain DENANTES/ Getty Images, p. 14; Gareth Fuller/ PA/ AP Images, pp. 14-15, 16 (ship lobby), 19 (step four); Angel Garcia/ Bloomberg/ Getty Images, p. 16; EQRoy, p. 17 (*Icon of the Seas*); Alvaro Victor, pp. 18-19; Jens Kalaene/ picture-alliance/ dpa/ AP Images, p. 19 (step one); Sina Schuldt/ picture-alliance/ dpa/ AP Images, p. 19 (step two); Bernd Wüstneck/ picture alliance/ Getty Images, p. 19 (step three); Christian Charisius/ picture alliance/ Getty Images, p. 19 (step five); GreenOak, pp. 19 (step six), 21, 23 (ship); Nancy Pauwels, p. 20; Aleksandr Dyskin, p. 20 (inset image); apiguide, pp. 22-23, 24.

24